STUDY
FOR
SPECIAL MINISTERS
OF
HOLY COMMUNION

CATHOLIC TRUTH SOCIETY
PUBLISHERS TO THE HOLY SEE
LONDON

Published in 1980 by the
Incorporated Catholic Truth Society
Publishers to the Holy See
38/40 ECCLESTON SQUARE
LONDON SW1V 1PD

Cum originali concordat John P. Dewis
Nihil obstat R. J. Cuming, D.D.
Imprimatur Ralph Brown, V.G.

ISBN 0 85183 306 3

PUBLISHED BY THE INCORPORATED CATHOLIC TRUTH SOCIETY, LONDON
AND PRINTED BY BURLEIGH PRESS LTD., BRISTOL BS2 0QL
Printed in England

CONTENTS

3

APPENDICES

CHAPTER 1

THE CHURCH AND THE PARISH

Introduction

On the 25th January 1973 Pope Paul VI issued an Instruction *"Immensae Caritatis"* which, among other things, permitted laymen and women to assist in the distribution of Holy Communion.

The thinking behind this document was the Church's intention to foster devotion to the Eucharist, and the Church, "moved by pastoral zeal and concern," issued the necessary laws to put this into practice.

To encourage devotion to the Eucharist the Church found it necessary to make provision for receiving Communion easier in places where it was either impossible or difficult to receive communion because of a lack of ministers. This could occur both in churches with large congregations or within a parish where, because of other duties, or a very large number of sick or house-bound people, the ministers would be depriving these parishioners of the spiritual consolation which they receive from holy communion.

"Immensae Caritatis" also covered the regulations concerning fasting before holy communion by the sick, and in what circumstances the faithful may receive holy communion a second time on the same day.

To enable large congregations to receive holy communion, and to enable the sick to receive holy communion more frequently, Pope Paul VI established special ministers for holy communion to assist the priest.

This is not something new. An ancient custom of the church was for the faithful to take holy communion home to sick relatives, and indeed even to give themselves holy communion during the week if no priest was available. So really what was introduced in 1973 was the revival of a very ancient custom in the Church.

1. The Church as the Body of Christ

St Paul used the expression the "Body of Christ" to describe the Church, the whole assembly of believers, living and dead in the Lord.

It was a favourite phrase of his by which he meant a single body or unit composed of the people of God united together through the Eucharist where all were fed with the living, risen Jesus, the "Head of the Body".

The Fathers of Vatican I Council in 1870 were attracted by the phrase "Body of Christ", but were also afraid of its vagueness, while the theologians of Vatican II developed the idea in relation to the Church, the "mystical Body of Christ", a development found also in the encyclicals *Satis Cognitum* and *Mystici Corporis* (CTS Do 266).

The Church is the living "Body of Christ" made up of people sharing a common faith and nourished by the living bread of the Eucharist. We have become accustomed, unfortunately, to associating the word "Church" with a building, losing the early Biblical connotation of Assembly or People of God, pilgrims on the way.

2. The Eucharist and the local Church

The Church is most aptly called the Body of Christ when the whole body of believers is united by means of the sacraments, and especially the Eucharist. Through the Eucharist the Church continually lives and grows. In the local churches the people of God are gathered and through the Body and Blood of the Lord the whole people of God are united. Every gathering of the people of God, under the ministry of the bishop, or the priest, representing the bishop, is a sign of the unity of the Mystical Body.

3. Special Ministries

At a Eucharistic celebration the faithful are seen as a sacred assembly—and should appear as one body, whether they are listening to God's word, taking part in prayers, and especially when together they offer the sacrifice and share in the Lord's table. Within the Eucharistic assembly there are certain special ministries, which in former times were carried out by clerics, but in recent years have been handed over to the laity. In the General

6

Instruction on the Roman Missal (CTS Do 455) these are listed as: the choir, the altar server, the special minister of holy communion, the reader, the psalmist, the commentator, the ushers, the collectors.

4. *Relationship between special minister of holy communion and the ministerial priesthood*

Distributing holy communion is always a priestly action—building up men into the Body of Christ, sanctifying the world by making men into the Sacrifice of Christ constantly consecrated in praise to the Father. This priestly function is the role of the Church as a whole and of each of her members, but can only attain its full and sacramental realization through the action of the ministerial, ordained priesthood. Without these priests the Church who is sacramental, in her very being, is unable to realize herself as the Body of Christ.

Any exercise of the Church's priestly role by the lay person is, therefore, always related to and dependent on the functioning of the ministerial priesthood which alone is the full sacramental expression of Christ the Priest living and acting in his Body, the Church. Whenever the priest exercises his priestly function, he is not only acting in his own individual name, but is 'actualising' the priesthood of the whole Church, including its lay members; but it is no part of the sacramental provision of the Church for the individual lay person to exercise directly and in its full sense the priesthood which is established in him by his baptism and confirmation. It does, however, remain possible for him to exercise it in a partial way and in conjunction with the ordained priest.

CHAPTER 2

THE HISTORICAL ASPECT

In the early Church the Eucharist was normally only celebrated on Sundays and Feast days. Consequently, from the earliest days of the Church the custom grew of the Christians taking home the

7

eucharistic bread and wine, and giving themselves holy communion at home during the week, whether they were sick or not.

Hippolytus in his "Apostolic Tradition" appeals to all Christians to fast before receiving holy communion at home. Further on in the same work he gives further directives to the Christians. For example, he asks that the Body and Blood of Christ should not be profaned by the pagans or animals.

Tertullian tells about the Eucharist being reserved and received in private houses. In *Ad uxorem* Tertullian refers to the difficulties a Christian would encounter in marrying a pagan, and how it would be necessary for the Christian to receive holy communion secretly.

Novatian, in the third century, writes in *De spectaculis* how it was reported that a certain believer came from a Eucharistic service and attended a pagan spectacle, with the Eucharist still in his pocket.

The custom of reserving and receiving the Eucharist at home continued up until the end of the eighth century, although even after that there are cases reported of the custom continuing right up to the early thirteenth century.

From these three well-known examples, and the fact that reservation of the Eucharist in churches was the exception rather than the rule up until the end of the eighth century, it is apparent that the Christians of the early Church often received holy communion from fellow Christians who were not priests.

Likewise, up to the end of the eighth century the common practice in the Church was for lay people to administer holy communion to the sick and, in homes where the Eucharist was reserved, for the sick to give themselves holy communion. It must be mentioned, however, that in some areas the bishops stressed that it was the obligation of priests to take holy communion to the sick or dying. From the late eighth century there are many statements by bishops which make it quite clear that administering holy communion to the sick was reserved to the priest alone.

While the custom of lay people taking holy communion to the sick declined from the eighth century onwards, there are traces of the custom continuing as late as the twelfth century. By the

8

fifteenth century respect for the Eucharist went so far that a lay person was not allowed even to touch the sacred host. The Church has, however, given permission for lay people to administer holy communion in a few cases during times of persecution, for example, in Mexico in 1927.

What is presented in *Immensae Caritatis* is therefore not something new, but rather an ancient custom of the Church which is being re-introduced for the benefit of the Church of the twentieth century.

CHAPTER 3

THE SPECIAL MINISTER AND THE PARISH

1. *Selection of Candidates*

The selection of persons to be special ministers of holy communion, and the determination whether in fact there is a necessity for such ministers, is primarily the responsibility of the parish clergy. It is recommended, however, that priests should consult the parish, the Parish Council, and, of course, the bishop.

The Church reminds bishops and priests that the person who is appointed to be a special minister of holy communion "should distinguish himself or herself by Christian life, faith and morals. Let him strive to be worthy of this great office; let him cultivate devotion to the holy Eucharist, and show himself as an example to the other faithful by his piety and reverence for this most holy Sacrament of the altar. Let no one be chosen whose selection may cause scandal among the faithful" (*Immensae Caritatis*).

It is not recommended that volunteers be called for when a parish is considering candidates for this ministry. To refuse the services of a volunteer is often very difficult. It is far easier, after due consultation, to approach possible candidates and ask them if they would be willing to serve the parish by offering themselves as candidates.

Immensae Caritatis lists an order from which suitable persons should be chosen: "reader, student of major seminary, male

9

religious, woman religious, catechist, man or woman." It is recommended that as far as possible the body of special ministers should represent a fair cross-section of the parish as regards class, ethnic origin, and sex, so that they may be seen as truly representative of the parish.

2. *The number of special ministers in a parish*

The number of special ministers to be appointed in a parish should be decided by the parish clergy in consultation with the parish council and the bishop. To avoid jealousy or strain on any particular individual I believe that no parish should have just one special minister, but it must be remembered that the local bishop's power to appoint special ministers who have not been instituted as acolytes is subject to there being a pastoral necessity for the appointment.

3. *The special minister at Mass*

Where special ministers assist a priest in the distribution of holy communion during Mass, the special ministers should take it in turn to assist at any particular Mass, so as to avoid any impression arising that a parish has only one special minister, or that a special minister is any more than that.

When a special minister is to assist in the distribution of holy communion during Mass, he or she must not fulfil any other liturgical function at that Mass, such as reader, server, cantor, because these are special ministries in their own right.

The choice of dress which a special minister should wear when assisting in the distribution of holy communion at a parish Mass is for the parish to decide. Some suggestions are cassock and cotta, an alb, a large shawl for women, or even simply ordinary clothes over which a cross is hung.

4. *Pastoral care of the special ministers*

Once the special ministers have been commissioned there is a danger that they will be abandoned to get on with their work. This should not be the case. It is suggested that once a month or every two months the parish clergy should get together with all the special ministers to talk over their work, to sort out difficulties, or even just in order to have a general get-together and discussion.

5. *Special ministers in schools, hospitals, etc.*
Sometimes chaplains of schools, hospitals, and other large institutions may feel the need of members of the staff to be commissioned to assist them in their work. In such situations the chaplain should approach the bishop.

6. *Celebrant at ceremony of commissioning special ministers*
The bishop is the normal celebrant when special ministers are being commissioned. In exceptional circumstances the bishop may delegate this authority.

When a special minister is required urgently, and for a specific occasion, a priest may commission a person there and then to help him distribute holy communion on that particular occasion. The Rite for Commissioning a Special Minister to Distribute Holy Communion on a Single Occasion, which should be used in these circumstances, will be found at appendix 5 of this booklet.

7. *Certificate of authority*
It is recommended that an annual certificate authorising the special minister to assist in distributing holy communion during Mass and outside Mass should be given to each commissioned person. An example of such a certificate will be found in the appendices to this booklet. The certificate could be signed by both the bishop and the parish priest at the ceremony of commissioning. The subsequent annual certificates need only be signed by the parish priest.

8. *When a special minister moves from one parish to another parish*
When a special minister moves from one parish to another parish he or she should not automatically continue as a special minister in the new parish. As can be seen from the annual certificate it is better if a person is commissioned to serve a specific parish. The parish priest of the new parish may, if he so wishes, avail of the services of the special minister. The final decision is reserved solely to the new parish priest if the suggested certificate procedure is adhered to.

11

CHAPTER 4

HOLY COMMUNION AND THE SICK

The instruction *Immensae Caritatis* of 1973, which gave local ordinaries the faculty to introduce special ministers, specifically mentions taking holy communion to the sick as one of the reasons for selecting special ministers of holy communion.

The Apostolic Constitution *Sacram Unctionem Infirmorum*, of 30th November 1972, reminds parish priests that they "should see to it that the sick and aged, even if not seriously sick or in imminent danger of death, be given every opportunity to receive the eucharist frequently and even daily, if possible, especially during the Easter season. They may receive communion at any hour" (Paragraph 46).

With the help of special ministers this instruction can be reasonably met in many if not most parishes. One of the most satisfying experiences a priest can have is to take holy communion to a sick person on a Sunday, or major feast day such as Christmas Day or Easter Sunday. By using the services of special ministers, especially when the special minister takes holy communion straight from Mass, the sick person is able to associate himself or herself with the Mass just celebrated.

There is no reason at all why a relative, or even a neighbour who is in contact with an elderly, or housebound, or sick person should not be commissioned solely for taking holy communion to that person.

A word of caution. Never send a special minister to a sick person without warning. What might seem the most natural thing to do may well upset an elderly, or housebound, or sick person. The most satisfactory way of starting off with special ministers taking holy communion to the sick at home would be for the priest one week to mention that a special minister would be calling with holy communion on Sundays. The following week the priest should go with the special minister, and introduce him or her. More often than not once the introduction has been made by the priest those confined to their homes will welcome the visit by the special minister.

It is not always so easy to have special ministers taking holy communion to patients in hospitals, or residents in Old People's Homes. Before special ministers start taking holy communion to either hospital patients or to residents in Old People's Homes it is recommended that the chaplain first discuss his plans with the nursing staff and the authorities. Normally the nursing staff and the authorities are most co-operative, especially when anything is being planned for the benefit of the patients. However, both the nursing staff and the hospital authorities get upset, if not annoyed, when a change in the system is introduced without their knowledge.

CHAPTER 5

THE PREPARATION OF THE SPECIAL MINISTER OF HOLY COMMUNION

Proper preparation for special ministers of holy communion is essential; it should be both a spiritual and practical one.

The minimum should be three talks or discussions, and the final preparation should be a day, or at least a half day, of recollection immediately prior to the ceremony of commissioning. These days of recollection could be organised on either a deanery or diocesan basis.

The aim of the talks or discussions should be to give the candidates first of all a deeper understanding of the Mass, and second to give them some practical preparation for carrying out their duties.

Each priest or catechist will have his or her own way of presenting the subject, but the following points at least should be covered in the initial preparation.

1. *The Eucharist and the Bible*
(a) The idea of sacrifice in the Bible.

13

(b) The idea of a meal in the Bible.
(c) The relationship between the Passover Meal and the Last Supper.
(d) The accounts of the institution of the Eucharist—Matthew 26: 26–29; Mark 14: 22–25; Luke 22: 14–20.
(e) The Eucharist in St Paul, especially 1 Corinthians 10 and 11.
(f) St John's Gospel, Chapter 6.

2. *The Theology of the Eucharist*

As a basis for talking about the theology of the Eucharist two documents are recommended:

1. "The Holy Eucharist"—the Encyclical Letter of Pope Paul VI, otherwise known as *Mysterium Fidei*, given in 1965 (CTS Do 355).

2. "The Instruction on the Worship of the Eucharistic Mystery", otherwise known as *Eucharisticum Mysterium* issued in 1967 (See Appendix 1).

There are many other books available on the theology of the Eucharist, but these two documents are recommended because they are relatively easy to follow, omit technical language, and are authoritative.

3. *The Rite of the Mass*

One talk should be given over to the Mass—its rites, and structures. Books recommended for this talk are:

1. *Communion*, by Sean Swayne, published by Veritas Publications, Dublin, 1974.

2. *The Church at Prayer—the Eucharist*, by A. G. Martimort, published by the Irish University Press, Shannon, Ireland, 1973. This book covers the Mass in some depth, and also takes in the history and development of the various rites.

3. *Christian Celebration—the Mass*, by J. D. Crichton, published by Geoffrey Chapman, London, 1975.

4. *A practical session*

The practical session should cover the following points:

1. Distributing the Sacred Host and Consecrated Wine.

14

2. Handling the chalice and purificator.
3. Purifying and care of chalice and ciborium.
4. How to break hosts when necessary.
5. Communion for the sick at home or in hospital.
6. Explanation of objects used in worship—chalice, paten, ciborium, purificator, lavabo towels, pall, chalice veil, tabernacle, sanctuary lamp.

Chapter 6

PREPARATION OF THE PARISH COMMUNITY

From comments made by priests it is clear that the acceptance or rejection of special ministers by the parish community does depend very much on how well the parish has been prepared for the introduction of special ministers into its life.

Opportunity must be taken some weeks before the special ministers are commissioned to prepare the people of the parish. The means of preparation are available to all priests, and they need to be used—sermons, newsletters, and prayers of the faithful. The one thing that should not need stressing, but nevertheless is stressed, is that if the preparation is to be done by preaching on the subject then all the parish clergy need to work together to ensure that all the parish is prepared.

The preparation of the parish community for the introduction of special ministers of holy communion should cover the following points at least:

1. The use of lay people in assisting in the distribution of holy communion is not something new, but is rather the revival of an ancient custom of the Church (see Chapter 2).
2. The special minister does not replace the priest, but rather assists him in his work. The priest will still visit the sick as usual but on Sundays the priest will have more time to give to the people before and after Mass; the priest will be able to give more time to prayer on Sundays—preparation before Mass and thanksgiving after Mass.

3. Using special ministers on Sundays and feast days means that a shorter time is taken up in distributing holy communion at Mass. This gives scope for a more prayerful celebration; the silent pause after holy communion need not be reduced to a mere token on the grounds that the first to receive holy communion have already been waiting anything up to ten minutes.

4. The use of special ministers makes possible more frequent holy communion for the sick and housebound, especially on Sundays. There would also be time to make the celebration of holy communion in the home more complete and prayerful, giving time for readings and reflection and for prayer with the sick person. Holy communion can be very moving when it is the parent, wife or husband who brings holy communion to the sick at home from the parish Mass on Sundays. In every case it forms a positive link between the community of Sunday worshippers and the sick and aged unable to participate fully in the Sunday liturgy.

5. Introducing special ministers into a parish enables the parish community to receive holy communion under both kinds more frequently. The General Instruction on the Roman Missal in commenting on communion under both kinds says: "The meaning of Communion is signified as clearly as possible when it is given under both kinds. In this form the meal-aspect of the Eucharist is more fully manifested, and Christ's intention that the new and eternal Covenant should be ratified in his blood is better expressed. Also the connection between the eucharistic meal and the heavenly banquet in the Father's kingdom becomes easier to see."

CHAPTER 7

ANNUAL RENEWAL OF COMMITMENT BY SPECIAL MINISTERS

About a week before Holy Week of each year it is recommended that all special ministers attend a day of recollection, before renewing their commitment. These days of recollection could be arranged by the diocese.

All special ministers should renew their commitment on Maundy Thursday each year at the Mass of the Lord's Supper before the priests and people of their parish. This, of course, means that a special minister is only commissioned for a year at a time. However, the value of limiting the time for which a person is commissioned is that should anything untoward occur during the year both the special minister and the parish priest have an opportunity to decide whether or not the special minister should continue his or her special role in the life of the parish.

Suggested rite of renewal of commitment by special ministers

The renewal should take place after the homily.
The special ministers stand in front of the parish priest who presides at the renewal.

PRIEST: Are you resolved to continue to undertake the office of special minister of holy communion for the service and growth of the Church?

MINISTERS: **I am.**

PRIEST: Are you resolved to continue to administer the holy eucharist with the utmost care and reverence?

MINISTERS: **I am.**

PRIEST: Are you resolved to continue to strive more earnestly than ever to live the Christian life, to give good example, and to take your faith more seriously?

MINISTERS: **I am.**

The special ministers then kneel. The priest continues:

PRIEST: Dear friends in Christ,
Let us pray with confidence to the Father; let us ask him to bestow his blessings on our brothers and sisters, chosen to be ministers of the Eucharist:

Merciful Father, creator and guide of your family, bless ✠ our brothers and sisters. May they faithfully give the bread of life to your people. Strengthened by

17

this sacrament may they come at last to the banquet of heaven.

We ask this through Christ our Lord.

MINISTERS: **Amen.**

PRIEST: You are authorised to continue to assist the priests and people of this parish in the distribution of holy communion until Maundy Thursday 19   . Sometime next Lent you must attend a day of prayer, and at the Mass of the Lord's Supper on Maundy Thursday you must renew your commitment before the priests and the people of this parish.

INSTRUCTION ON THE WORSHIP OF EUCHARISTIC MYSTERY

EUCHARISTICUM MYSTERIUM, 25th May, 1967

1. *Recent documents of the Church concerning the Mystery of the Eucharist*

The mystery of the Eucharist is the true centre of the sacred liturgy and indeed of the whole Christian life. Consequently the Church, guided by the Holy Spirit, continually seeks to understand and to live the Eucharist more fully.

In our own day the Second Vatican Council has stressed several important aspects of this mystery.

In the *Constitution on the Liturgy* (CTS Do 386) the Council recalled certain facts about the nature and importance of the Eucharist. It established principles for the reform of the rites of the sacrifice of the Mass so as to encourage the full and active participation of the faithful in the celebration of this mystery. It also extended the practice of concelebration and communion under both kinds.

In the *Constitution on the Church* (CTS Do 349) the Council showed the close and necessary connection between the Eucharist and the mystery of the Church. Other documents of the Council frequently stressed the important role of the eucharistic mystery in the life of the faithful. They showed its power to reveal the meaning of man's work, and indeed of all created nature, since in it "natural elements, refined by man, are changed into the glorified Body and Blood."

Pope Pius XII had prepared the way for many of these statements of the Council, especially in the Encyclical Letter *Mediator Dei* (CTS Do 270) while Pope Paul VI in the Encyclical Letter *Mysterium Fidei* (CTS Do 355) has recalled the importance of certain aspects of eucharistic doctrine, of the real presence of

Christ in particular and the worship due to this sacrament even outside the Mass.

2. *The need to retain an overall view of the teaching contained in these documents*

In recent years, then, certain aspects of the traditional teaching on this mystery have been the subject of deeper reflection throughout the Church, and have been presented with new zeal for the greater spiritual benefit of the faithful. Undertakings and research in various fields, particularly the liturgical and biblical, have greatly assisted this process.

From the doctrine contained in these documents it is necessary to formulate practical norms which will show the Christian people how to act in regard to this sacrament so as to pursue that knowledge and holiness which the Council has set before the Church.

It is important that the mystery of the Eucharist should shine out before the eyes of the faithful in its true light. It should be considered in all its different aspects, and the real relationships which, as the Church teaches, are known to exist between these various aspects of the mystery should be so understood by the faithful as to be reflected in their lives.

3. *The principal points of doctrine in these documents*

Among the doctrinal principals concerning the Eucharist formulated in these documents of the Church, the following should be noted as having a bearing upon the attitude of Christians towards this mystery, and, therefore, as falling within the scope of this Instruction.

(a) "The Son of God in the human nature which he united to himself redeemed man and transformed him into a new creation (cf. Gal. 6:15; 2 Cor. 5:17) by overcoming death through his own death and resurrection. For by giving his spirit he mystically established as his body his brethren gathered from all nations. In that body the life of Christ is communicated to those who believe; for through the sacraments they are joined in a mysterious yet real way to the Christ who suffered and is glorified" (*Constitution on the Church*, n. 7).

Therefore "Our Saviour at the Last Supper on the night when he was betrayed instituted the eucharistic sacrifice of his Body and Blood so that he might perpetuate the sacrifice of the cross throughout the centuries till his coming. He thus entrusted to the Church, his beloved spouse, a memorial of his death and resurrection: a sacrament of love, a sign of unity, a bond of charity, a paschal meal in which Christ is eaten, the mind filled with grace and a pledge of future glory given to us" (*Constitution on the Sacred Liturgy*, n. 47).

Hence the Mass, the Lord's Supper, is at the same time and inseparably:

a sacrifice in which the sacrifice of the cross is perpetuated;

a memorial of the death and resurrection of the Lord, who said "do this in memory of me" (Lk. 22:19);

a sacred banquet in which, through the communion of the Body and Blood of the Lord, the People of God share the benefits of the Paschal Sacrifice, renew the New Covenant which God has made with man once for all through the Blood of Christ, and in faith and hope foreshadow and anticipate the eschatological banquet in the kingdom of the Father, proclaiming the Lord's death "till his coming".

(b) In the Mass, therefore, the sacrifice and sacred meal belong to the same mystery—so much so that they are linked by the closest bond.

For in the sacrifice of the Mass Our Lord is immolated when "he begins to be present sacramentally as the spiritual food of the faithful under the appearances of bread and wine." It was for this purpose that Christ entrusted this sacrifice to the Church, that the faithful might share in it both spiritually, by faith and charity, and sacramentally, through the banquet of Holy Communion. Participation in the Lord's Supper is always communion with Christ offering himself for us as a sacrifice to the Father.

(c) The celebration of the Eucharist which takes place at Mass is the action not only of Christ, but also of the Church. For in it Christ perpetuates in an unbloody manner the sacrifice offered on the cross, offering himself to the Father for the world's salvation through the ministry of priests. The Church, the spouse and minister of Christ, performs together with him the role of priest and victim, offers him to the Father and at the same time makes a total offering of herself together with him.

Thus the Church, especially in the great Eucharistic Prayer, together with Christ, gives thanks to the Father in the Holy Spirit for all the blessings which he gives to men in creation and especially in the Paschal Mystery, and prays to him for the coming of his kingdom.

(d) Hence no Mass, indeed no liturgical action, is a purely private action, but rather a celebration of the Church as a society composed of different orders and ministries in which each member acts according to his own order and role.

(e) The celebration of the Eucharist in the sacrifice of the Mass is the origin and consummation of the worship shown to the Eucharist outside Mass. Not only are the sacred species which remain after the Mass derived from the Mass, but they are preserved so that those of the faithful who cannot come to Mass may be united to Christ, and his sacrifice celebrated in the Mass, through sacramental communion received with the right dispositions.

Consequently the eucharistic sacrifice is the source and the summit of the whole of the Church's worship and of the Christian life. The faithful participate more fully in this sacrament of thanksgiving, propitiation, petition and praise, not only when they whole-heartedly offer the sacred victim, and in it themselves, to the Father with the priest, but also when they receive this same victim sacramentally.

(f) There should be no doubt in anyone's mind "that all the faithful ought to show to this most holy sacrament the worship which is due to the true God, as has always been the custom of the Catholic Church. Nor is it to be adored any the less because it was instituted by Christ to be eaten." For even in the reserved sacrament he is to be adored because he is substantially present there through that conversion of bread and wine which, as the Council of Trent tells us, is most aptly named transubstantiation.

(g) The mystery of the Eucharist should therefore be considered in all its fullness, not only in the celebration of Mass but also in devotion to the sacred species which remain after Mass and are reserved to extend the grace of the sacrifice.

These are the principles from which practical rules are to be drawn to govern devotion due to the sacrament outside Mass and its proper relation to the right ordering of the sacrifice of the Mass according to the mind of the Second Vatican Council and the other documents of the Apostolic See on this subject.

4. *The general intention of this instruction*

For this reason the Consilium set up to implement the Constitution of the Liturgy, on the instructions of His Holiness Pope Paul VI, has prepared an Instruction setting out such practical rules of this nature as may be suitable for the present situation.

The particular purpose of these rules is not only to emphasize the general principles of how to instruct the people in the Eucharist, but also to make more readily intelligible the signs by which the Eucharist is celebrated as the memorial of the Lord and worshipped as a permanent sacrament in the Church.

For although this sacrament has this supreme and unique feature, that the author of holiness is himself present in it, nevertheless, in common with the other sacraments, it is the symbol of a sacred reality and the visible form of an invisible grace. Consequently the more intelligible the signs by which it is celebrated and worshipped, the more firmly and effectively it will enter into the minds and lives of the faithful.

I. SOME GENERAL PRINCIPLES OF PARTICULAR IMPORTANCE IN INSTRUCTING THE PEOPLE OF GOD IN THE MYSTERY OF THE EUCHARIST

5. *What is required of pastors who are to give instruction about this mystery?*

Suitable catechesis is essential if the mystery of the Eucharist is to take deeper root in the minds and lives of the faithful.

To convey this instruction properly, pastors should not only bear in mind the many aspects of the Church's teaching, as contained in the documents of the magisterium, but in their hearts and in their lives they must endeavour to penetrate more deeply the Church's spirit in this matter (*spiritum Ecclesiae . . . altius penetrare*). Only then will they readily perceive which of the many facets of this mystery best suits the needs of the faithful at any one time.

While recalling all that was said above in n. 3, one should take special note of what follows below.

6. *The mystery of the Eucharist as the centre of the entire life of the Church*

The catechesis of the eucharistic mystery should aim to help the faithful to realize that the celebration of the Eucharist is the true centre of the whole Christian life both for the universal Church and for the local congregation of that Church. For "the other sacraments, as indeed every ministry of the Church and every work of the apostolate, are linked with the Eucharist and are directed towards it. For the Eucharist contains the entire spiritual good of the Church, namely, Christ himself, our Passover and living bread, offering through his flesh, living and life-giving in the Spirit, life to men who are thus invited and led on to offer themselves, their labours and all created things together with him."

The Eucharist both perfectly signifies and wonderfully effects that sharing in God's life and unity of God's people by which the Church exists. It is the summit of both the action by which God sanctifies the world in Christ, and the worship which men offer to Christ and which through him they offer to the Father in the Spirit. Its celebration "is the supreme means by which the faithful come to express in their lives and to manifest to others the mystery of Christ and the true nature of the Church".

7. *The mystery of the Eucharist as the focal point of the local Church*

It is through the Eucharist that "the Church continually lives and grows. This Church of Christ is truly present in all legitimate local congregations of the faithful which, united with their pastors, are called churches in the New Testament. These are, each in its own region, the new people, called by God in the Holy Spirit and in all fullness (cf. 1 Th. 1:5). In them the faithful are gathered by the preaching of Christ's Gospel and the mystery of the Lord's Supper is celebrated, 'so that through the Body and Blood of the Lord the whole brotherhood is united.'" "Every gathering around the altar under the sacred ministry of the bishop or of a priest who takes the place of the bishop is a sign of that charity and 'unity of the Mystical Body, without which there can be no salvation.'" "In these communities, though they may often be small and poor or living amongst the diaspora, Christ is present, by whose power the one holy catholic and apostolic Church is united. For 'the partaking of the Body and Blood of Christ has no less an effect than to change us into what we have received.'"

8. The Eucharistic Mystery and Christian Unity

In addition to those things which concern the ecclesial community and the individual faithful, pastors should pay particular attention to that part of her doctrine in which the Church teaches that the memorial of the Lord, celebrated according to his will, signifies and effects the unity of all who believe in him.

As the Decree on Ecumenism of the Second Vatican Council (CTS Do 351) declares, the faithful should be led to a proper appreciation of the values which are preserved in the eucharistic tradition according to which our brethren of the other Christian confessions have continued to celebrate the Lord's Supper. For while "they call to mind the death and resurrection of the Lord in the Holy Supper, they profess that it signifies life in communion with Christ and await his coming in glory." But those who have preserved the sacrament of Order, "united with the bishop, have access to God the Father through the Son, the Word incarnate, who suffered and is glorified, by the outpouring of the Holy Spirit, and attain communion with the Blessed Trinity, becoming 'sharers of the divine nature' (2 Pet. 1:4). And so through the celebration of the Lord's Eucharist in these individual churches the Church of God is built up and grows, and their communion is manifested through concelebration."

It is above all in the celebration of the mystery of unity that all Christians should be filled with sorrow at the divisions which separate them. They should therefore pray earnestly to God that all disciples of Christ may daily come closer to a proper understanding of the mystery of the Eucharist according to his mind, and may so celebrate it as to become sharers in the Body of Christ, and so become one body (cf. 1 Cor. 10:17) "linked by the very bonds by which he wishes it to be constituted."

9. *The different modes of Christ's presence*

In order that they should achieve a deeper understanding of the mystery of the Eucharist, the faithful should be instructed in the principal ways in which the Lord is present to his Church in liturgical celebrations.

He is always present in a body of the faithful gathered in his name (cf. Mt. 18:20). He is present, too, in his Word, for it is he who speaks when the Scriptures are read in Church.

In the sacrifice of the Eucharist he is present both in the person of the minister, "the same now offering through the ministry of the priest who formerly offered himself on the cross," and above all under the species of the Eucharist. For in this sacrament Christ is present in a unique way, whole and entire, God and man, substantially and continuingly. This presence of Christ under the species "is called 'real' not in an exclusive sense, as if the other kinds of presence were not real, but *par excellence*."

10. *The connection between the Liturgy of the Word and the Liturgy of the Eucharist*

Pastors should therefore "carefully teach the faithful to participate in the whole Mass," showing the close connection between the liturgy of the Word and the celebration of the Lord's Supper, so that they can see clearly how the two constitute a single act of worship. For "the teaching of the Word is necessary for the very administration of the sacraments, in as much as they are sacraments of faith, which is born of the Word and fed by it." This is especially true of the celebration of Mass, in which it is the purpose of the liturgy of the Word to develop the close connection between the preaching and hearing of the Word of God and the eucharistic mystery.

When therefore the faithful hear the Word of God, they should realize that the wonders it proclaims culminate in the Paschal

Mystery, of which the memorial is sacramentally celebrated in the Mass. In this way the faithful will be nourished by the Word of God which they have received and in a spirit of thanksgiving will be led on to a fruitful participation in the mysteries of salvation. Thus the Church is nourished by the bread of life which she finds at the table both of the Word of God and of the Body of Christ.

11. *The priesthood common to all the faithful and the ministerial priesthood in the Celebration of the Eucharist*

The more clearly the faithful understand the place they occupy in the liturgical community and the part they have to play in the eucharistic action, the more conscious and fruitful will be the active participation which is proper to that community.

Catechetical instruction should therefore explain the doctrine of the royal priesthood to which the faithful are consecrated by rebirth and the anointing of the Holy Spirit.

Moreover there should also be further explanation of the role in the celebration of the Eucharist of the ministerial priesthood which differs from the common priesthood of the faithful in essence and not merely in degree. The part played by others who exercise a ministry in the Eucharist should also be explained.

12. *The nature of active participation in the Mass*

It should be made clear that all who gather for the Eucharist constitute that holy people which, together with the ministers, plays its part in the sacred action. It is indeed the priest alone, who, acting in the person of Christ, consecrates the bread and wine, but the role of the faithful in the Eucharist is to recall the passion, resurrection and glorification of the Lord, to give thanks to God, and to offer the immaculate victim not only through the hands of the priest, but also together with him; and finally, by receiving the Body of the Lord, to perfect that communion with God and among themselves which should be the product of participation in the sacrifice of the Mass. For the faithful achieve a more perfect participation in the Mass when, with proper dispositions, they receive the Body of the Lord sacramentally in the Mass itself, in obedience to his words "take and eat".

Like the passion of Christ itself, this sacrifice, though offered for all, "has no effect except in those united to the passion of Christ by faith and charity . . . To these things it brings a greater or less benefit in proportion to their devotion."

All these things should be explained to the faithful, so that they may take an active part in the celebration of the Mass both by their personal devotion and by joining in the external rites, according to the principles laid down in the *Constitution on the Liturgy*, which have been further determined by the Instruction *Inter Oecumenici* (CTS Do 348) of 26 September 1964 and the Instruction *Musicam Sacram* (CTS Do 387) of 5 March 1967, and through the Instruction *Tres abhinc annos* of 4 May 1967.

13. *The influence of the Eucharist on the daily lives of the faithful*

What the faithful have received by faith and sacrament in the celebration of the Eucharist should have its effect on their way of life. They should seek to live joyfully and gratefully by the strength of this heavenly food, sharing in the death and resurrection of the Lord. And so everyone who has participated in the Mass should be "eager to do good works, to please God, and to live honestly, devoted to the Church, putting into practice what he has learnt, and growing in piety." He will seek to fill the world with the Spirit of Christ and 'in all things, in the very midst of human affairs" to become a witness of Christ.

For no "Christian community can be built up unless it has as its basis and pivot the celebration of the holy Eucharist. It is from this therefore that any attempt to form a community must begin."

14. *Teaching children about the Mass*

Those who have charge of the religious instruction of children, especially parents, parish priests and teachers, should be careful when they are introducing them gradually to the mystery of salvation, to give emphasis to instruction on the Mass. Instruction about the Eucharist, while being suited to the age and abilities of the children, should aim to convey the meaning of the Mass through the principal rites and prayers. It should also explain the place of the Mass in participation in the life of the Church.

All this should be borne in mind especially when children are being prepared for first communion so that the first communion may be seen as the full incorporation into the Body of Christ.

15. Catechesis of the Mass should take the Rites and Prayers as its starting point

The Council of Trent prescribes that pastors should frequently "either themselves or through others, expound some part of what is read at Mass and, among other things, explain something of the mystery of this sacrament."

Pastors should therefore gently lead the faithful to a full understanding of this mystery of faith by suitable catechesis. This should take as its starting point the mysteries of the liturgical year and the rites and prayers which are part of the celebration. It should clarify their meaning and especially that of the great eucharistic prayer, and should lead the people to a profound understanding of the mystery which these signify and accomplish.

II. SOME GENERAL NORMS CONCERNING THE CELEBRATION OF THE MEMORIAL OF THE LORD IN THE COMMUNITY OF THE FAITHFUL

16. The common unity to be shown in the celebration

Since through baptism "there is neither Jew nor Greek, slave nor freeman, male nor female," but all are one in Christ Jesus (cf. Gal. 3:28), the assembly which most fully portrays the nature of the Church and its role in the Eucharist is that which gathers together the faithful, men and women, of every age and walk of life.

The unity of this community, having its origin in the one bread in which all share (cf. 1 Cor. 10:17), is arranged in hierarchical order. For this reason it is necessary that "each person, performing his role as a minister or as one of the faithful, should do all that the nature of the action and the liturgical norms require of him, and only that."

The outstanding example of this unity may be seen "in the full and active participation of the entire people of God . . . in the same Eucharist, in a single prayer, around the one altar where the bishop presides, accompanied by his priests and ministers."

(The remainder of this document is not relevant to the subject being covered in this booklet, and has been omitted.)

INSTRUCTION ON FACILITATING SACRAMENTAL EUCHARISTIC COMMUNION IN PARTICULAR CIRCUMSTANCES

IMMENSAE CARITATIS, 25th January, 1973

Christ the Lord has left to the Church, his spouse, a testament of his immense love. The wonderful gift of the Eucharist, which is the greatest gift of all, demands that this important mystery should be increasingly better known and its saving power more fully shared. With the intention of fostering devotion to the Eucharist—the summit and centre of Christian worship—the Church, moved by pastoral zeal and concern, has issued suitable laws and appropriate documents.

Present day conditions, however, demand that, while the greatest reverence toward this Sacrament is constantly maintained, easier access to holy communion should be made possible. Thus the faithful, by sharing more fully in the fruits of the sacrifice of the Mass, may dedicate themselves more readily and effectively to God and to the good of the Church and of mankind.

First of all, provision must be made lest reception of communion become impossible or difficult because of insufficient ministers. The sick must not be deprived of spiritual consolation by being impeded from receiving holy communion because of the law of fast, which they may not be able to observe even though it is already very moderate. Finally, it seems appropriate to determine in what circumstances the faithful who ask to receive sacramental communion a second time on the same day may be permitted fittingly to do so.

After study of the recommendations of certain episcopal conferences, the following norms are issued:

1. *Special ministers for the distribution of Holy Communion*
There are various circumstances in which a lack of sufficient

ministers for the distribution of Holy Communion can occur:

during Mass because of the size of the congregation or a particular difficulty in which a celebrant finds himself;

outside Mass, when it is difficult because of distance to take communion, especially viaticum, to the sick in danger of death, or when the very number of the sick, especially in hospitals and similar institutions, requires a number of ministers.

So that the faithful, who are in the state of grace and who with an upright and pious disposition wish to share in the sacred banquet, may not be deprived of this sacramental help and consolation, it has seemed appropriate to the Pope to establish special "extraordinary" ministers, who may give holy communion to themselves and to other members of the faithful under the following specific conditions:

i. Local ordinaries have the faculty to permit a qualified person individually chosen as a special minister for a specific occasion or for a time or, in case of necessity, in a permanent way, either to give the Eucharist to himself or to other members of the faithful or to take it to the sick who are confined to their homes. This faculty may be used when

  (a) there is no priest, deacon, or acolyte;
  (b) these ministers are prevented from administering holy communion because of another pastoral ministry or because of ill health or advanced age;
  (c) the number of the faithful requesting holy communion is such that the celebration of Mass or the distribution of the Eucharist outside Mass would be unduly prolonged.

ii. Local ordinaries also have the faculty to permit individual priests exercising their sacred office to appoint a qualified person to distribute holy communion on a specific occasion, in cases of genuine need.

iii. The above mentioned local ordinaries may delegate these faculties to auxiliary bishops, episcopal vicars, and episcopal delegates.

iv. The qualified person to whom Nos. i and ii refer shall be designated according to the following order: reader, student of major seminary, male religious, woman religious, catechist, man or woman. This order, however, may be changed according to the prudent judgment of the local ordinary.

v. In oratories of religious communities of either sex the office of distributing holy communion in the circumstances described in No. i may properly be given to a male superior who does not have major orders or to a woman superior or to their respective vicars.

vi. If time permits, it is fitting that the qualified person individually chosen by the local ordinary for administering holy communion, as well as the person appointed by a priest having the faculty spoken of in No. ii, should receive the mandate according to the rite appended to this instruction; they are to distribute holy communion according to the liturgical norms.

Since these faculties are granted only for the spiritual good of the faithful and for cases of genuine necessity, priests are to remember that they are not thereby excused from the task of distributing the Eucharist to the faithful who legitimately request it, and especially not from giving communion to the sick.

The person who has been appointed to be a special minister of holy communion must be duly instructed and should distinguish himself or herself by Christian life, faith, and morals; striving to be worthy of this great office, cultivating devotion to the holy Eucharist and acting as an example to the other faithful by piety and reverence for this most holy Sacrament of the altar. Let no one be chosen whose selection may cause scandal among the faithful.

2. *Extension of the faculty to receive Holy Communion twice on the same day*

According to the discipline now in force, the faithful are permitted to receive holy communion a second time:

on the evening of Saturday or of the day preceding a holy-day of obligation, when they intend to fulfil the precept of assisting at Mass, even though they have already received holy communion in the morning of that same day;

at the second Mass of Easter and at one of the Masses celebrated on Christmas Day, even if they have already received holy communion at the Mass of the Easter Vigil or at the midnight Mass of Christmas;

at the evening Mass of Holy Thursday, even if they have received holy communion at the earlier chrism Mass.

In addition to these circumstances, there are similar occasions which suggest that holy communion may fittingly be received twice in the same day. It is thus necessary to determine more precisely the reasons for the new faculty.

The norm which the Church, as a provident Mother, has introduced according to venerable custom and included in canon law by which the faithful are permitted to receive holy communion only once a day remains intact. It is not permitted to be set aside merely from motives of devotion. A simple desire for repeated reception of holy communion should be answered by explaining that the power of the sacrament by which faith, charity, and other virtues are nourished, strengthened, and expressed is the greater to the extent that one more devoutly approaches the sacred table. From the liturgical celebration the faithful should go out to the works of charity, piety, and apostolic action so that "they may hold fast by their conduct and life to what they have received by faith and the Sacrament."

Special circumstances, however, can occur when the faithful who have already received holy communion, or even priests who have already celebrated Mass, may be present at a community celebration. They may receive holy communion again in the following instances:

1. at those Masses in which the sacraments of baptism, confirmation, anointing of the sick, orders, and matrimony are celebrated, and at a Mass at which first communion is received;

2. at Masses at which a church or altar is consecrated; at Masses of religious profession or for the conferring of a canonical mission;

3. at the following Masses for the dead: the funeral Mass, the Mass celebrated after notification of death, the Mass on the day of final burial, and the Mass on the first anniversary;

4. at the principal Mass celebrated in the cathedral or in the parish on the feast of Corpus Christi and on the day of a parochial visitation; at the Mass celebrated by the major superior of a religious community on the occasion of a canonical visitation, special meetings, or chapters;

5. at the principal Mass of a Eucharistic or Marian Congress, international or national, regional or diocesan;

6. at the principal Mass of any congress, sacred pilgrimage, or preaching mission for the people;

7. in the administration of viaticum, in which communion may also be given to the relatives and friends of the sick person.

8. Besides the cases mentioned above, local ordinaries may also grant permission *ad actum* to receive holy communion twice on the same day as often as they judge it truly justified by reason of genuinely special circumstances, according to the norm of this instruction.

3. *Mitigation of the Eucharistic fast for the sick and the aged*

First, a person to whom viaticum is administered in danger of death is not bound by any law of fasting; this norm remains in effect. Likewise in force is the concession already granted by Pius XII whereby "the sick, even if not confined to bed, may take non-alcoholic drinks and medicines in either liquid or solid form before the celebration of Mass and the reception of the Eucharist without any restriction of time."

In the case of foods and drinks taken for the purpose of nutrition, tradition is to be respected: the Eucharist should be received, as Tertullian said, "before any food" so as to indicate the excellence of the sacramental food.

In order to appreciate the dignity of the Sacrament and to prepare with joy for the coming of the Lord, a time of silence and recollection before the reception of holy communion is appropriate. In the case of the sick, however, it will be sufficient sign of piety and reverence if, for a brief period of time, they turn their minds to the greatness of the mystery. The period of time of the eucharistic fast or abstinence from food and alcoholic drink is

34

reduced to approximately one quarter of an hour, for the following persons:

1. the sick in hospitals or in their own homes, even if they are not confined to bed;
2. the faithful advanced in age who must remain at home because of age or who are living in a home for the elderly;
3. sick priests, even if not confined to bed, and elderly priests, who wish to celebrate Mass or receive holy communion;
4. persons looking after the sick and the aged as well as those relatives of the sick and aged wishing to receive holy communion with them, whenever they are unable to observe the fast of one hour without inconvenience.

4. *Piety and reverence to the Blessed Sacrament when the Eucharist is placed on the hands of the faithful*

Since the instruction *Memoriale Domini* was published three years ago, some episcopal conferences have sought the faculty from the Apostolic See to allow the minister of holy communion to place the eucharistic species in the hands of the faithful. As that instruction recalled, "The precepts of the Church and the documents of the Fathers amply testify that the deepest reverence and the greatest prudence have been shown with regard to the Holy Eucharist" and should continue to be shown. Especially in this manner of receiving holy communion, some points indicated by experience should be most carefully observed.

The greatest diligence and care should be taken particularly with regard to fragments which may break off the hosts. This applies to the minister and to the recipient whenever the sacred host is placed in the hands of the communicant.

Before initiating the practice of holy communion in the hand, a suitable instruction and catechesis on Catholic doctrine is necessary concerning both the real and permanent presence of Christ under the eucharistic species and the reverence due to this sacrament.

It is necessary to instruct the faithful that Jesus Christ is the Lord and Saviour and that the same worship and adoration given to God is owed to him present under the sacramental signs.

The faithful should be counselled not to omit a sincere and fitting thanksgiving after the eucharistic banquet, in accord with each one's particular ability, state, and duties. So that participation in this heavenly table may be worthy and profitable, the value and effects deriving from it for the individual and the community must be pointed out. In this way the customary attitude of the faithful will reveal reverence, foster intimate love for the Father of the household who gives us "our daily bread" and lead to a living relationship with Christ of whose flesh and blood we partake.

APPENDIX 3

INSTRUCTION ON HOLY COMMUNION AND WORSHIP OF THE EUCHARIST OUTSIDE MASS

EUCHARISTIAE SACRAMENTUM, 21st June, 1973
(Extracts)

The relationship between Eucharistic worship outside Mass and the Eucharistic celebration

The celebration of the eucharist is the centre of the entire Christian life, both for the Church universal and for the local congregations of the Church. "The other sacraments, all the ministries of the Church, and the works of the apostolate are united with the eucharist and are directed toward it. For the holy eucharist contains the entire spiritual treasure of the Church, that is, Christ himself, our passover and living bread. Through his flesh, made living and life-giving by the Holy Spirit, he offers life to men, who are thus invited and led to offer themselves, their work, and all creation together with him."

"The celebration of the eucharist in the sacrifice of the Mass," moreover, "is truly the origin and the goal of the worship which is shown to the eucharist outside Mass." Christ the Lord "is offered in the sacrifice of the Mass when he becomes present sacramentally as the spiritual food of the faithful under the appearance of bread and wine." And, "once the sacrifice is offered and while the eucharist is reserved in churches and oratories, he is truly

Emmanuel, 'God with us'. He is in our midst day and night; full of grace and truth, he dwells among us."

No one therefore may doubt "that all the faithful show this holy sacrament the veneration and adoration which is due to God himself, as has always been customary in the Catholic Church. Nor is the sacrament to be less the object of adoration because it was instituted by Christ the Lord to be received as food."

In order to direct and to encourage devotion to the sacrament of the eucharist correctly, the eucharistic mystery must be considered correctly, the eutharistic mystery must be considered in all its fullness, both in the celebration of Mass and in the worship of the sacrament which is reserved after Mass to extend the grace of the sacrifice.

The relationship between Communion outside Mass and the Sacrifice
Sacramental communion received during Mass is the more perfect participation in the eucharistic celebration. The eucharistic sign is expressed more clearly when the faithful receive the body of the Lord from the same sacrifice after the communion of the priest. Therefore, recently baked bread, for the communion of the faithful, should ordinarily be consecrated in every eucharistic celebration.

The faithful should be encouraged to receive communion during the eucharistic celebration itself.

Priests, however, are not to refuse to give communion to the faithful who ask for it even outside Mass.

In fact it is proper that those who are prevented from being present at the community's celebration should be refreshed with the eucharist. In this way they may realize that they are united not only with the Lord's sacrifice but also with the community itself and are supported by the love of their brothers and sisters.

Pastors should see that an opportunity to receive the eucharist is given to the sick and aged, even though not gravely sick or in imminent danger of death, frequently and, if possible, daily, especially during the Easter season. It is lawful to minister communion under the appearance of wine to those who cannot receive the consecrated bread.

The faithful should be instructed carefully that, even when they receive communion outside Mass, they are closely united with the sacrifice which perpetuates the sacrifice of the cross. They are sharers in the sacred banquet in which "by communion in the body and blood of the Lord the people of God share in the blessings of the paschal sacrifice, renew the new covenant once made by God with men in the blood of Christ, and by faith and hope prefigure and anticipate the eschatological banquet in the kingdom of the Father, proclaiming the death of the Lord until he comes."

The time of Communion outside Mass
Communion may be given outside Mass on any day and at any hour. It is proper, however, to determine the hours for giving communion, with a view to the convenience of the faithful, so that the celebration may take place in a fuller form and with greater spiritual benefit.

Nevertheless:

(a) on Holy Thursday, communion may be given only during Mass; communion may be brought to the sick at any hour of the day;

(b) on Good Friday communion may be given only during the celebration of the Passion of the Lord; communion may be brought to the sick who cannot participate in the celebration at any hour of the day;

(c) on Holy Saturday communion may be given only as viaticum.

The minister of Communion
It is, first of all, the office of the priest and the deacon to minister holy communion to the faithful who ask to receive it. It is most fitting, therefore, that they give a suitable part of their time to this ministry of their order, depending on the needs of the faithful.

It is the office of an acolyte who has been properly instituted to give communion as a special minister when the priest and deacon are absent or impeded by sickness, old age, or pastoral ministry or when the number of the faithful at the holy table is so great that the Mass or other service may be unreasonably protracted.

The local Ordinary may give other special ministers the faculty to give communion whenever it seems necessary for the pastoral benefit of the faithful and a priest, deacon, or acolyte is not available.

The place of Communion outside Mass

The place where communion outside Mass is ordinarily given is a church or oratory in which the eucharist is regularly celebrated or reserved or a church, oratory, or other place where the local community regularly gathers for the liturgical assembly on Sundays or other days. Communion may be given, however, in other places, including private homes, when it is a question of the sick, prisoners, or others who cannot leave the place without danger or serious difficulty.

Regulations for giving Communion

When communion is given in a church or oratory, a corporal is to be placed on the altar, which is already covered with a cloth. A communion plate is to be used.

When communion is given in other places, a suitable table is to be prepared and covered with a cloth; candles are also to be provided.

The minister of communion, if he is a priect or deacon, is to be vested in an alb, or a surplice over a cassock, and a stole.

Other ministers should wear either the liturgical vesture which may be traditional in the region or their vestment which is appropriate for this ministry and has been approved by the Ordinary.

The eucharist for communion outside a church is to be carried in a pyx or other covered vessel; the vesture of the minister and the manner of carrying the eucharist should be appropriate and in accord with local circumstances.

In giving communion the custom of placing the particle of consecrated bread on the tongue of the communicant is to be maintained because it is based on a tradition of several centuries.

Episcopal conferences, however, may decree, their actions having been confirmed by the Apostolic See, that communion may also be given in their territories by placing the consecrated bread in the hands of the faithful, provided there is no danger of

39

irreverence or false opinions about the eucharist entering the minds of the faithful.

The faithful should be instructed that Jesus Christ is Lord and Saviour and that, present in the sacrament, he must be given the same worship and adoration which is to be given to God.

In either case, communion must be given by the competent minister, who shows the particle of consecrated bread to the communicant and gives it to him, saying, *The body of Christ*, to which the communicant replies *Amen*.

In the case of communion under the appearance of wine, the regulations of the instruction *Sacramentali Communione* of June 29, 1970, are to be followed exactly.

Fragments which may remain after communion are to be reverently gathered and placed in a ciborium or in a vessel with water.

Likewise, if communion is given under the appearance of wine, the chalice or other vessel is to be washed with water.

The water used for cleansing the vessels may be drunk or poured out in a suitable place.

Dispositions for Communion

The eucharist continuously makes present among man the paschal mystery of Christ. It is the source of every grace and of the forgiveness of sins. Nevertheless, those who intend to receive the body of the Lord must approach it with a pure conscience and proper dispositions of soul if they are to receive the effects of the paschal sacrament.

On this account the Church prescribes "that no one conscious of mortal sin, even though he seems to be contrite, may go to the holy eucharist without previous sacramental confession." In urgent necessity and if no confessor is available, he should simply make an act of perfect contrition with the intention of confessing individually, at the proper time, the mortal sins which he cannot confess at present.

It is desirable that those who receive communion daily or very often go to the sacrament of penance at regular intervals, depending on their circumstances.

Besides this, the faithful should look upon the eucharist as an antidote which frees them from daily faults and keeps them from mortal sins; they should also understand the proper way to use the penitential parts of the liturgy, especially at Mass.

Communicants are not to receive the sacrament unless they have fasted for one hour from solid food and beverages, with the exception of water.

The period of the eucharistic fast, that is, abstinence from food or alcoholic drink, is reduced to about a quarter of an hour for:

(1) the sick who are living in hospitals or at home, even if they are not confined to bed;

(2) the faithful of advanced age, even if not bedridden, whether they are confined to their homes because of old age or live in a nursing home;

(3) sick priests, even if not bedridden, or elderly priests, whether they are to celebrate Mass or to receive communion;

(4) persons who care for the sick or aged, and the family of the sick or aged, who wish to receive communion with them, when they cannot conveniently observe the fast of one hour.

The union with Christ, to which the sacrament is directed, should be extended to the whole of Christian life. Thus the faithful, constantly reflecting upon the gift they have received, should carry on their daily work with thanksgiving, under the guidance of the Holy Spirit, and should bring forth fruits of rich charity.

So that they may continue more easily in the thanksgiving which is offered to God in an excellent manner through the Mass, it is recommended that each one who has been refreshed by communion should remain in prayer for a period of time.

APPENDIX 4

RITE OF COMMISSIONING SPECIAL MINISTERS OF HOLY COMMUNION

Persons authorized to distribute holy communion in special circumstances should be commissioned by the local Ordinary or his delegate according to the following rite. The rite should take place in the presence of the people during Mass or outside Mass.

During Mass

In the homily the celebrant first explains the reason for this ministry and then presents to the people those chosen to serve as special ministers, using these or similar words:

Dear friends in Christ,

Our brothers and sisters N. and N. are to be entrusted with administering the eucharist, with taking communion to the sick, and with giving it as viaticum to the dying.

The celebrant pauses, and then addresses the candidates:

In this ministry, you must be examples of Christian living in faith and conduct; you must strive to grow in holiness through this sacrament of unity and love. Remember that, though many, we are one body because we share the one bread and one cup.

As ministers of holy communion be, therefore, especially observant of the Lord's command to love your neighbour. For when he gave his body as food to his disciples, he said to them: "This is my commandment, that you should love one another as I have loved you."

After the address the candidates stand before the celebrant, who asks them these questions:

Are you resolved to undertake the office of giving the body and blood of the Lord to your brothers and sisters, and so serve to build up the Church?

R̃. **I am.**

Are you resolved to administer the holy eucharist with the utmost care and reverence?

R̃. **I am.**

All stand. The candidates kneel and the celebrant invites the faithful to pray:

Dear friends in Christ,

Let us pray with confidence to the Father; let us ask him to bestow his blessings on our brothers and sisters, chosen to be ministers of the eucharist:

Pause for silent prayer. The celebrant then continues:

Merciful Father,
creator and guide of your family,
bless ✠ our brothers and sisters N. and N.
May they faithfully give the bread of life
to your people.
Strengthened by this sacrament,
may they come at last
to the banquet of heaven.
We ask this through Christ our Lord.

R̸. **Amen.**

The general intercessions should include an intention for the newly-commissioned ministers.

In the procession at the presentation of gifts, the newly-commissioned ministers carry the vessels with the bread and wine, and at communion may receive the eucharist under both kinds.

Outside Mass

When the people are assembled an appropriate song is sung. The celebrant greets the people. There normally follows a short Liturgy of the Word. The readings and chants are taken, either in whole or in part, from the liturgy of the day or from those given in Appendix 7.

The rite continues as above.

Finally, the celebrant blesses the people and dismisses them in the usual way. The rite concludes with an appropriate song.

APPENDIX 5

RITE OF COMMISSIONING A SPECIAL MINISTER TO DISTRIBUTE HOLY COMMUNION ON A SINGLE OCCASION

A person who, in a case of real necessity, is authorized to distribute holy communion on a single occasion should normally be commissioned according to the following rite.

During the breaking of the bread and the commingling, the

person who is to distribute holy communion comes to the altar and stands before the celebrant. After the **Lamb of God** the priest blesses him/her with these words:

**Today you are to distribute
the body and blood of Christ
to your brothers and sisters.
May the Lord bless ✠ you, N.**

R̷. Amen.

When the priest has himself received communion in the usual way, he gives communion to the minister of the eucharist. Then he gives him/her the paten or other vessel with the hosts. They then go to give communion to the people.

APPENDIX 6

RITE OF DISTRIBUTING HOLY COMMUNION BY A SPECIAL MINISTER

A special minister of holy communion should wear the vestments customary in the country, or clothing in keeping with this sacred ministry.

In distributing holy communion during Mass, the minister holds the host slightly raised and says:

The body of Christ.

The communicant answers: **Amen,** and receives it.

After all have received communion, the minister of the eucharist cleanses his/her fingers over the paten and, if necessary, washes them and then returns to his/her place.

In administering the chalice, the minister holds the chalice out to the communicant and says:

The blood of Christ.

The communicant answers: **Amen,** and, taking the chalice, drinks from it.

After all have received communion, the minister of the eucharist places the chalice on the altar and returns to his/her place.

In distributing holy communion outside Mass, the special minister is to follow the rite given in the Roman Ritual: *Holy Communion and Worship of the Eucharist outside Mass.*

BIBLICAL TEXTS FOR USE IN THE RITE OUTSIDE MASS

OLD TESTAMENT READINGS

1. Genesis 14:18–20   He brought bread and wine.
2. Exodus 16:2–4, 12–15   I will rain down bread for you from the heavens.
3. Exodus 24:3–8   This is the blood of the Covenant that the Lord has made with you.
4. Deuteronomy 8:2–3, 14–16   He fed you with manna which neither you nor your fathers had known.
5. 1 Kings 19:4–8   Strengthened by that food he walked until he reached the mountain of God.
6. Proverbs 9:1–6   Eat my bread, drink the wine I have prepared for you.

NEW TESTAMENT READINGS

1. Acts 2:42–47   The faithful all lived together and owned everything in common.
2. Acts 10:34, 37–43   We have eaten and drunk with him after his resurrection.
3. 1 Corinthians 10:16–17   That there is only one loaf means that, though there are many of us, we form a single body.
4. 1 Corinthians 11:23–26   Until the Lord comes, every time you eat this bread and drink this cup, you proclaim his death.
5. Hebrews 9:11–15   The blood of Christ can purify our inner self from dead actions.

RESPONSORIAL PSALMS

1. Psalm 22. R 1
   Ry. The Lord is my shepherd: there is nothing I shall want.

2. Psalm 33:2–11. R 9
   R̥. Taste and see that the Lord is good.
3. Psalm 77:3–4, 23–25, 54. R 24
   R̥. The Lord gave them bread from heaven.
4. Psalm 109:1–4. Alt. R v 4
   R̥. A priest for ever,
      a priest like Melchizedek of old,
      Christ the Lord offered bread and wine.
   Alt. R̥. You are a priest for ever,
      a priest like Melchizedek of old.
5. Psalm 115:12–13, 15–18. R 1 Cor 10:16
   R̥. The blessing-cup we bless
      is a communion in the blood of Christ.
   Alt. R̥. Alleluia!
6. Psalm 144:10–11. 15–18. R 16
   R̥. You open wide your hand, Lord, grant the desires of all
      who live.
7. Psalm 147:12–15, 19–20 R Jn 6:58
   R̥. Anyone who eats this bread will live for ever.

ALLELUIA VERSE BEFORE THE GOSPEL
1. John 6:56 He who eats my flesh and drinks my blood lives
   in me and I live in him, says the Lord.
2. John 6:57 As I, who am sent by the living Father, myself
   draw life from the Father, so whoever eats me will draw life
   from me, says the Lord.
3. John 6:35 I am the bread of life. He who comes to me will
   never be hungry; he who believes in me will never thirst, says
   the Lord.
4. John 6:51 I am the living bread which has come down from
   heaven, says the Lord. Anyone who eats this bread will live
   for ever.

GOSPEL READINGS
1. Mark 14:12–16, 22–26 This is my body. This is my blood.
2. Luke 9:11–17 They all ate as much as they wanted.
3. Luke 24:13–35 They recognized him at the breaking of bread.

4. John 6:1–15 Jesus gave out as much as was wanted to all who were sitting ready.
5. John 6:24–35 He who comes to me will never be hungry; he who believes in me will never thirst.
6. John 6:41–51 I am the living bread which has come down from heaven.
7. John 6:51–58 My flesh is real food and my blood is real drink.
8. John 21:1–14 Jesus took the bread and gave it to them.

APPENDIX 8

SAMPLE CERTIFICATE OF AUTHORITY

DIOCESE OF ....

PARISH OF ....

(TOWN) ....

(NAME) ....

IS HEREBY AUTHORISED TO ASSIST IN THE DISTRIBUTION OF HOLY COMMUNION AT MASS AND TO TAKE HOLY COMMUNION TO THE SICK OF THE PARISH, UNTIL MAUNDY THURSDAY 19.........................

BISHOP   PARISH PRIEST

APPENDIX 9

BIBLIOGRAPHY

1. *Sacramentum Mundi—An Encyclopedia of Theology*, 6 Vols, Editor: Karl Rahner (Burns and Oates, London, 1969).

2. *Vatican Council II—the Conciliar and Post Conciliar Documents*, General Editor: Austin Flannery (Costello Publishing Co, U.S.A., 1975).

3. *The Church at Prayer*, 2 Vols, Editor: A. G. Martimort (Irish University Press, 1968, 1971).

4. *The Bible and the Liturgy*, by Jean Danielou (Darton, Longman and Todd, London, 1960).

5. *The Eucharist in the New Testament*, by J. Delorme and others (Geoffrey Chapman, London, 1964).

6. *The Early Liturgy*, by J. A. Jungman (Darton, Longman and Todd, London, 1959).

7. *Eucharistic Theology*, by Joseph M. Powers (Burns and Oates, London, 1968).

8. *Christian Celebration—The Mass*, by J. D. Crichton (Geoffrey Chapman, London, 1975).

9. *Communion—The New Rite of Mass*, by Sean Swayne (Veritas Publications, Dublin, 1974).